# BIGGEST NAMES IN SPORTS

# MOOKIE BETTS

## BASEBALL STAR

by Greg Bates

FOCUS READERS

# WWW.FOCUSREADERS.COM

Copyright © 2019 by Focus Readers, Lake Elmo, MN 55042. All rights reserved. No part of this book may be reproduced or utilized in any form or by any means without written permission from the publisher.

Focus Readers is distributed by North Star Editions:
sales@northstareditions.com | 888-417-0195

Produced for Focus Readers by Red Line Editorial.

Photographs ©: Kathy Willens/AP Images, cover, 1, 21; Elise Amendola/AP Images, 4–5, 27; David J. Phillip/AP Images, 7, 9; Mike Strasinger, 10–11, 13; Cliff Welch/Icon Sportswire, 15; Mike Janes/Four Seam Images/AP Images, 16–17; Ken Babbitt/Four Seam Images/AP Images, 19; Chris Szagola/AP Images, 22–23; Michael Dwyer/AP Images, 25; Red Line Editorial, 29

**Library of Congress Cataloging-in-Publication Data**
Library of Congress Cataloging-in-Publication Data is available on the Library of Congress website.

**ISBN**
978-1-64185-317-0 (hardcover)
978-1-64185-375-0 (paperback)
978-1-64185-491-7 (ebook pdf)
978-1-64185-433-7 (hosted ebook)

Printed in the United States of America
Mankato, MN
October, 2018

# ABOUT THE AUTHOR

Greg Bates is a freelance sports journalist based in Green Bay, Wisconsin. He has covered the Green Bay Packers for a decade. He has written for outlets such as *USA Today Sports Weekly*, the Associated Press, Green Bay Packers Yearbook, and USA Hockey. Greg and his wife have a young daughter.

# TABLE OF CONTENTS

# CHAPTER 1

# TOP OF THE WORLD

It was Game 1 of the 2018 World Series. Betts and the Boston Red Sox were facing the Los Angeles Dodgers. The series opened at Fenway Park in front of 38,000 screaming Red Sox fans.

In his first at bat, Betts hit a single. That was no surprise to the Boston crowd.

**Betts hits a single in Game 1 of the 2018 World Series.**

During the regular season, Betts had led Major League Baseball (MLB) with an outstanding .346 batting average.

Up next was Red Sox outfielder Andrew Benintendi. That's when Betts showed off his speed. Betts stole second base, putting himself into **scoring position**. When Benintendi singled, Betts came around to score the first run of the series.

Betts scored another run in the fifth inning to give the Sox a 4–3 lead. They never trailed again. Boston won the game 8–4. That gave them a 1–0 lead in the best-of-seven series.

Betts had another solid performance in Game 2. With the Red Sox trailing

Betts rounds the bases after getting a hit in Game 2 of the World Series.

1–2 in the fifth inning, Betts hit a single to center field. Three batters later, J. D. Martinez hit a single that brought Betts home. The Red Sox went on to win the game 4–2. They now led the series 2–0.

When the series shifted to Los Angeles, Betts struggled. Game 3 turned out to be an 18-inning marathon. Betts didn't have any hits, and Boston lost 3–2. Game 4 was another tough one for Betts. Even so, the Red Sox found a way to win. They were now one victory away from a title.

## AN UNUSUAL NAME

Mookie's real name is Markus Lynn Betts. His mom was happy when she realized his initials formed MLB. Those letters also refer to Major League Baseball. Betts got the nickname "Mookie" from his parents. They were big fans of Atlanta Hawks basketball star Mookie Blaylock. Ever since Betts was a little kid, the nickname "Mookie" has stuck with him.

Betts and the Red Sox celebrate a World Series victory.

In Game 5, the Sox were clinging to a 2–1 lead in the sixth inning. That's when Betts hammered a home run to left field. Boston went on to win the game 5–1. The Red Sox were World Series champions! For Betts, it was the first title of a promising career.

# CHAPTER 2

# A NATURAL ON THE DIAMOND

Mookie Betts was born on October 7, 1992, in Nashville, Tennessee. When Mookie was little, he loved sports. He competed on several travel teams. His dad drove him to two or three baseball tournaments every month. When Mookie got to John Overton High School, he was a star on the baseball team.

**Mookie Betts throws the ball to first base during a game with John Overton High School.**

He hit .549 as a junior, with 37 RBIs and 24 stolen bases. Those numbers started to attract the interest of colleges. During his senior year, Mookie kept doing well at the plate. He received an honorable mention for the Louisville Slugger High School All-American list.

## ALL IN THE FAMILY

Mookie's uncle, Terry Shumpert, played in the major leagues for 14 years. He even played with the Red Sox for a short time. When Mookie was 11 years old, his uncle often took him to the baseball field after school. Shumpert would hit balls to him. That gave Mookie a chance to work on his fielding. He learned a lot about baseball from his uncle.

Mookie Betts swings for the fences during a high school game.

Mookie wasn't just a great baseball player. He also excelled at basketball. As a senior, he was named the most valuable player (MVP) of his district.

Mookie was also an outstanding bowler. He averaged a score of 230 out of 300. As a senior, he was named the Tennessee Bowler of the Year. His high score that year was an impressive 290.

Even though Mookie was great at basketball and bowling, he focused on baseball. He was a talented shortstop. And thanks to his skill, several colleges went after him.

Mookie decided he would play at the University of Tennessee. However, a **scout** with the Red Sox had been watching Mookie for a while. He thought Mookie had what it took to play in the major leagues someday. In 2011, the Red Sox

A 17-year-old Mookie Betts runs to first base during a 2010 game.

selected Mookie in the fifth round of the MLB **draft**. Now Mookie had a big decision to make. Would he go to college, or would he sign with the Red Sox?

# CHAPTER 3

# MOVING UP THROUGH THE MINORS

**M**ookie Betts knew he wasn't good enough to play in the majors right after high school. That meant he had two choices. He could play college ball. Or, he could sign with the Red Sox. But if he signed with Boston, he would start in the minor leagues to develop his skills. Betts decided to skip college and turn pro.

**Betts watches the ball sail in a 2011 minor league game.**

The minor league system has several levels. Betts started out at the lowest level. However, he soon moved up thanks to his solid hitting. While playing for the Salem Red Sox, he won some major awards. He was named the Offensive Player of the Year. He was also named **Breakout** Player of the Year.

In 2014, Betts climbed up to the Double-A level. He entered the season ranked as one of the top 100 **prospects** in baseball. Betts had one of the best batting averages in the Eastern League.

Next, he moved up to Triple-A. That's the highest level in the minor leagues. With the Pawtucket Red Sox, Betts racked

Betts sprints around the bases as a member of the Lowell Spinners during a 2012 minor league game.

up the hits. He impressed the coaches so much that he was called up to the big leagues.

Betts was valuable to the Red Sox because he could play two of the three outfield positions. He made his MLB **debut** on June 29, 2014. The game was against Boston's biggest rival, the New York Yankees. In his first career at bat, Betts grounded out. But in his second at bat, he hit a single to center field.

## PERFECT GAMES

Baseball isn't the only sport that Betts plays professionally. He is also a member of the Professional Bowlers Association (PBA). He's such a good bowler he rolled a perfect game in a PBA event. That would be impressive for any bowler. It's even more impressive for one who is also a pro baseball player.

Betts takes a swing in his first major league game.

Betts ended up playing in 52 games for the Red Sox that year. His dream of becoming a major leaguer had come true. But Betts wanted to do more than just play in the majors. He wanted to be a star.

# CHAPTER 4

# BECOMING A STAR

In the 2015 season, Mookie Betts made the **starting lineup** on Opening Day. He even hit a home run in the first game of the season. That was just a preview of good things to come. Betts cranked out another 17 homers that year. And once again, he had a great batting average.

**Betts waits for a pitch on Opening Day in 2015.**

In 2016, Betts had his breakout year. In fact, he was one of the top players in all of baseball. Betts showed his unique combination of power and speed. He finished second in the American League in batting average, hits, and runs. He was also a finalist for the league's MVP award.

The Red Sox reached the **postseason** in 2016. However, they fell to the Cleveland Indians. It was a tough loss for Betts and his teammates. But they were determined to make it back the next year.

By 2017, Betts had proven that he was one of the best young players in the league. And for the second year in a row, he was named to the All-Star team.

Betts steals second base during a 2016 game against the Yankees.

At the end of the year, Betts led the Red Sox in runs scored, stolen bases, home runs, and RBIs. But Betts was more than just a great offensive player. He also played extremely well in the outfield.

Betts won his second consecutive Gold Glove Award in 2017. That award is given to the league's best defensive player at each position.

Betts had another great season in 2018. In fact, he was a big reason why the Red Sox were the best team in the majors that year. Boston finished the regular

## BOWLING FOR A CAUSE

When Betts isn't playing baseball, he likes to help the community. For instance, he has hosted Mookie's Big League Bowl. In this event, Red Sox teammates bowl for a good cause. The money they raise is given to charities. These charities help improve the lives of children and families in the Boston area.

The crowd erupts after Betts hits a game-winning homer in the 10th inning against the Minnesota Twins in 2018.

season with an incredible 108 wins. And they didn't stop there. The team cruised to a World Series victory over the Los Angeles Dodgers. Betts and the Red Sox were champions!

# MOOKIE BETTS

- Height: 5 feet 9 inches (175 cm)
- Weight: 180 pounds (82 kg)
- Birth date: October 7, 1992
- Birthplace: Nashville, Tennessee
- High school: John Overton (Nashville, Tennessee)
- Minor league teams: GCL Red Sox (2011); Lowell Spinners (2012); Greenville Drive (2013); Salem Red Sox (2013); Portland Sea Dogs (2014); Pawtucket Red Sox (2014)
- MLB team: Boston Red Sox (2014–)
- Major awards: World Series champion (2018); American League MVP (2018); American League batting champion (2018); Gold Glove Award (2016, 2017, 2018); Silver Slugger Award (2016, 2018)

Portland

Lowell

Boston

Pawtucket

Nashville

Greenville

# FOCUS ON
# MOOKIE BETTS

*Write your answers on a separate piece of paper.*

**1.** Write a sentence that describes the main ideas from Chapter 1.

**2.** What are the advantages of playing college sports before going pro? Can you think of any disadvantages?

**3.** Other than baseball, what two sports was Betts best at in high school?

    **A.** golf and track
    **B.** soccer and basketball
    **C.** basketball and bowling

**4.** Why didn't Betts play baseball for the University of Tennessee?

    **A.** because he suffered an injury after finishing high school
    **B.** because he was not good enough to play on the team
    **C.** because he started playing baseball professionally

*Answer key on page 32.*

# GLOSSARY

**breakout**
Having to do with a sudden success.

**debut**
First appearance.

**draft**
A system that allows teams to acquire new players coming into a league.

**postseason**
A set of games played after the regular season to decide which team will be the champion.

**prospects**
Players who are likely to be successful in the future.

**scoring position**
When a baseball player is on second or third base. From this position, a base hit will usually allow the runner to score.

**scout**
A person whose job involves looking for talented young players.

**starting lineup**
A list of people who will play from the beginning of a game. The list usually includes the team's best players.

# TO LEARN MORE

## BOOKS

Bryant, Howard. *Legends: The Best Players, Games, and Teams in Baseball*. New York: Penguin, 2015.

Kelley, K. C. *Boston Red Sox*. New York: AV2 by Weigl, 2018.

Tustison, Matt. *12 Reasons to Love the Boston Red Sox*. North Mankato, MN: 12-Story Library, 2016.

## NOTE TO EDUCATORS

Visit **www.focusreaders.com** to find lesson plans, activities, links, and other resources related to this title.

# INDEX

Answer Key: **1.** Answers will vary; **2.** Answers will vary; **3.** C; **4.** C